Rachel Carson
Protecting the Natural World

Darleen Ramos

Boston, Massachusetts
Chandler, Arizona
Glenview, Illinois
Upper Saddle River, New Jersey

Illustrations
Opener, 1, 4, 7, 10, 11, 13, 14, 15 Meryl Treatner; 3 Joe LeMonnier.

Photographs
Every effort has been made to secure permission and provide appropriate credit for photographic material.
The publisher deeply regrets any omission and pledges to correct errors called to its attention in subsequent editions.

Unless otherwise acknowledged, all photographs are the property of Pearson Education, Inc.

Photo locators denoted as follows: Top (T), Center (C), Bottom (B), Left (L), Right (R), Background (Bkgd)

2 U.S. Fish and Wildlife Service; 8 Comstock/Thinkstock; 9 Jupiterimages/Thinkstock; 12 ©Zacarias Pereira da Mala/
Shutterstock.

ISBN-13: 978-0-328-67601-9
ISBN-10: 0-328-67601-2

2 3 4 5 6 V0FL 16 15 14 13 12

A Friend of Nature

What do you think of when you hear the word *scientist*? Do you picture a person in a white coat working in a lab? Not all scientists work in labs. Some work outside studying plants and animals. Rachel Carson was a scientist and writer. She wrote about how people, animals, and plants are all connected to each other.

Carson studied the animals that live in the sea. She was one of the first **environmentalists**. She wrote about how important it is to keep our water, soil, and air clean. Her most important work describes how certain chemicals can harm living things.

Young Carson

Rachel Carson was born on a farm in Springdale, Pennsylvania, in 1907. As a child,

Springdale is in western Pennsylvania, far from the ocean.

she and her mother spent many hours outside enjoying nature. They explored the woods and the meadows. Carson was very curious. She liked to watch how insects and birds behaved. After exploring, Carson and her mother would talk about what they saw.

Carson also loved exploring little streams and a large nearby river called the Allegheny. But she had bigger dreams. She had read many stories about the ocean, and she wanted to see it. However, the closest ocean, the Atlantic, was hundreds of miles away. Carson hoped that she would see it someday.

A Child Writer

Carson had other interests when she was a child—reading and writing. She especially enjoyed reading stories from *St. Nicholas* magazine. This magazine was published for children. Some of its stories were even written by children.

When Carson was ten years old, she sent the magazine a story she wrote herself. It was called "A Battle in the Clouds." At the time, many Americans were fighting in a war. Her story was about a pilot. Carson was thrilled when the magazine published her story. It was so good that she even won a prize for it!

Young Carson drew pictures to go with her first stories.

Carson sent more of her stories to *St. Nicholas*. The magazine published four of them in all. Her last story to the magazine was a nature story. It was about going bird-watching with her dog. Carson was proud of having the stories published. She decided to be a writer when she grew up.

At school, Carson was always an excellent student. She graduated first in her high school class. The next step was college. Her family wanted to help Carson fulfill her dreams. To help pay for the high cost of college, her parents sold some of their farmland.

Off to College

Carson attended Pennsylvania College for Women in Pittsburgh. It was close to home. But unlike Springdale, Pittsburgh was a huge city with many factories. At the time, Pittsburgh was known for having the worst air **pollution** in the country.

In the 1920s, the city's main **industry** was steel. Steel mills burned coal to make steel, and smokestacks pumped soot from the coal into the air. The result was dirty air, polluted with coal dust. Sometimes the air was so thick with dust that it dimmed the sunlight. Even worse, people breathed in the dirty air and some became sick.

Pittsburgh's steel mills in the early 1900s

Carson studied hard at college.

Since Carson wanted to become a writer, she took English classes in college. She found time to write for the school newspaper and magazine. She often wrote about the ocean. Since she had never seen the ocean, she had to use her imagination to describe life under the sea.

All students at the college had to take some science classes. Carson chose biology, or the study of living things—plants and animals. Much to her surprise, she liked her biology classes. They reminded her of exploring the woods as a child.

Becoming a Scientist

Carson's interest in biology was because of her teacher, Mary Scott Skinker. Skinker took the class on field trips to places such as Cook State Forest. On hikes, they studied animals that lived in creeks and woods. The class made Carson want to understand more about nature.

College was a busy time for Carson. She studied both English and science. She knew she had to focus on one or the other. She could pick science, but there were few women scientists in the 1920s. It was a difficult decision.

Carson made up her mind to become a scientist. She still loved to write, but she decided to focus on zoology, the study of animal life. She graduated from college in 1929.

Carson loved her class's field trips to study animal life.

After college, Carson returned home for the summer. She had good news for her family. She had been accepted into a program to study **marine** life with other scientists.

As industries and cities grow, pollution can worsen.

Carson was going to study life in the sea!

While she was home, Carson noticed how dirty and brown the Allegheny River was now. It even smelled bad. Local power plants were to blame. They dumped waste into the Allegheny and released smoke, polluting the water and air. Carson never forgot the pollution in Pittsburgh and Springdale. One day she would work to teach others how people can harm the environment.

Carson at Woods Hole

The Ocean, at Last

Carson's summer study program was in Woods Hole, Massachusetts. She had never been so far from home. Woods Hole is near the Atlantic Ocean. For the first time, Carson could see, hear, and smell all the things she had written about!

Carson and other scientists spent several weeks learning about marine animals. She watched creatures in the water and on the shore, finding tiny animals on the rocks or clinging to seaweed. The things she learned would help her later in her life.

A Writer and a Scientist

After her studies, Carson got a job with the United States government. She wrote scripts for a radio show called "Romance Under the Waters." The shows taught listeners about fish and other marine life. Carson was happy. She was getting paid to write about her favorite subject—the ocean.

At the same time, Carson wrote newspaper and magazine articles about nature. Readers liked how she combined information about biology with beautiful descriptions. These articles proved that Carson was more than a scientist. She was a good writer, too. A book publisher asked her to write a book.

Nature Writer

Carson finished her first book, *Under the Sea Wind*, in 1941. In it she wrote about the daily lives of a sandpiper named Blackfoot and an eel named Anguilla. There is also a tiny mackerel fish named Scomber. Scomber hatches from an egg and grows up to join a school of other fish.

The book describes where the animals travel, how they hunt, and how they escape death. Along the way, they meet many different sea animals. No one could describe the beauty of the sea like Carson.

In the 1950s, Carson wrote two more books about marine life—*The Sea Around Us* and *The Edge of the Sea*. She made a difficult subject easy to read. Both books became bestsellers.

One of Carson's books told about the daily life of a sandpiper.

Planes were used to spray DDT on crops.

Concerns About Chemicals

In the late 1950s, Carson found a new concern. A friend, Olga Owens Huckins, wrote to Carson about a strange problem. Recently, a farmer had sprayed a field near her friend's home in Massachusetts with DDT. DDT was a powerful **pesticide** that was used on farm crops to kill insects that ate plants.

A few days after the spraying, Huckins found many dead birds on her land. Huckins thought the DDT could have caused the birds' deaths. She asked Carson to look into the problem.

A Book With a Message

Carson did her research. She learned that pesticides such as DDT harmed other things in the environment, not just harmful insects. Carson wanted to warn the public about the dangers of pesticides. In 1962, she wrote her most famous book, *Silent Spring.*

Carson's book told how poisonous pesticides moved up the **food chain**. Animals that ate plants sprayed with pesticides could get sick. People could also get sick if they ate these plants or animals. Pesticides also polluted the water and hurt animals and people. The chemicals could cause terrible diseases such as cancer or even death.

Silent Spring shocked many people. The government took action. Thanks to Carson's book, DDT was banned. The use of other types of pesticides was limited.

Carson died in 1964, but her words are still important. She taught people about the need to protect the environment. Because of Carson and other environmentalists, we now have laws that protect our air, water, and wildlife.

Carson knew that farm workers were at a high risk of getting sick from DDT because they worked close to the poisonous chemicals.

Glossary

environmentalist a person concerned about protecting the air, soil, and water around us

food chain a series of living things in which each living thing is food for the next living thing in the series

industry all the businesses that provide one kind of product

marine having to do with the sea

pesticide a chemical used to destroy insect pests

pollution harmful material that dirties the air, soil, or water